TABLE OF CONTENTS

PREFACE

Every season in this book is a season I have lived through -- some loud, some lonely, some full of growth I didn't even want. These pages came from plenty of time behind steel doors and bars, jail walls, and moments that humbled me into silence. These pages hold the version of me that was learning, breaking, rebuilding, and becoming. I hope that as you move through each season, you recognize something familiar, something true, something that speaks to your own experiences. Ultimately, I hope something in here reminds you that we keep changing, even when we don't notice. That we get to bloom again. Fall again. Freeze and thaw. And start over as many times as we need to.

Wherever you are in your journey, I'm honored you're here with me.

INTRODUCTION

In the county jail, there is an unspoken mathematic equation called the "two for one".

It means that the time doubled for however many actual days you served in jail.

For instance, six months spent in jail would count as twelve months time served.

Alot can happen within that timeframe and that includes enduring the four seasons.

This small book of original pieces represent just that –

living through all four seasons in poetic prose.

WINTER

Time Collapse

So what now?
I've had to face my biggest fears
After losing everything, I'm still here
And I'm not speaking of material things
I'm talking about my girls
They literally were my world
I reflect back to my deepest losses
How heavy the stakes my mistakes have costed
They seem to carry more weight as I get older
Cuz I realize how much time is behind me
When I look over my shoulder
Time is kinda slow in jail
But in the free world,
An hour passes by in the blink of an eye
In whatever case, I ain't getting no younger
The things I once valued at sixteen (16)
Don't mean as much to me as they did,
When I was a kid…
May all my past relationships Rest In Peace
May the groans of my heart eventually find relief
From affliction I shift my focus back to victory
Cuz I've got no other choice but to step into
Who I'm meant to be – in order to live freely
I lift my head up & widen my stride
Still having full meltdowns lowkey on the inside
Still grieving what I thought I had needed to survive
Thank God for the experiences that keep me alive
So what now?
I'll just keep living like the old heads used to say
Only this time around, I'm asking God to show me the way.

Higher Power

There is a beautiful overcast outside the cell window

The energy of Oya burns through my soul windows

I'm so hot with fire, I need water to cool down

The electricity from the earth shoots current from the ground

My mind is gone with the wind; I'm trynna reel it back in

With anger being my opponent, I refuse to let it win

The soreness of my body hurts mo' better when I stretch

I prefer the tightness of my muscles over the pressure in my chest

I could feel a million emotions in 1 day; that's what exhausts me

Disassociating or overreacting – both are costly

I pay attention to those that help me stay afloat

Bless those who speak life & ignore the ones that don't

The battlefield of the mind is real & so are the spirits that kill

God blessed me with the strength of a warrior, but also the power to heal

So I reverse the curse that my ancestors brought upon me

Give thanks to this day that grace & mercy has overcome me.!

Ghetto Psalm 100

Lemme vent for a minute

This is a rat infested jail – I ain't never seen nothing like it

Man y'all hell – the inmates be snitching MORE than the police do

And they're in the cell with you! Snitching is the main intention

But what is there to gain? Except a name as an informant

Talents lying dormant cuz you focused on some other shit

That you ain't got nothing to do with – Like Calloway ass

Nice/nasty MF and she must keep a bunch of peanut butter

Cuz she a rat like a MF ! While her minions –

That don't seem to form their own opinions;

Her followers be ready to swallow up whatever she feeds them

Pick out a new girl that she don't fancy and then tries to read 'em

Pettiness on the lowest level – I can't wait to get released

I'm nothing like these rodents Lord please set me free !

You don't know how to encourage me & its okay Mommy. It wasn't meant for you to do that – you were only meant to raise me. And between you & the Father, y'all made me the strongest warrior. Yes, I was birth from a woman in the flesh but I am NOT human. I do NOT belong to this earth. I come from somewhere else in the universe. I am an infinte being; not a human being. So this is not my home & dare I say: This is NOT where I belong. Even understanding these things, I don't fully understand my purpose here. Did I reincarnate here? They say that we choose to be reincarnated. Why would I want to relive this traumatic experience? Cuz I know I've been here before. It feels all too familiar. My essence exists in a place where there's no space or time. Just pure essence. So this human body that I possess must be the vessel that I'm supposed to use to do my work. My work is quite unorthodox though – I have the ability to break someone down & build them back up in the same breath. My vibrational energy is very fluid on the spectrum. Outside of my own ill actions, I can see how I would end up in such a low vibrational facility; doing the work of an alchemist. And still, I feel all of the aches & pains that a natural human would. My alchemy is not perfect! Perhaps, that's why I was brought to the jailhouse. Maybe it was meant for me to perfect my practice by way of learning and teaching simultaneously. In any event, once I've mastered what I've come here to do, I will transcend out of this vessel and I will be off to my next lifetime mission. Or will I even have another lifetime? In the meantime (and between time), let me continue my journey to figure out THIS lifetime.

– Godspeed Be with Me

SPRING

Spiritual Reset

Crying is literally an energy ting

It brings cleansing to the soul

Adding prayer is like a synergy ting

Then you exhaust & recharge two-fold

In the time of exhaustion, you must meditate on right tings

For the strength of your mental depend 'pon it

Joy & pain are like yin & yang

They really are both one & the same

Opposites sides of the token

You can't call it either way

Cuz when all is said & spoken,

God will have His way

The best ting is to manifest the next ting

To be the blessing that you need

Praying, fasting, crying…

The Living God moves through you when you do all three.

Divine Design

The world broke me down

God built me back up

Everytime I'm knocked down

He tells me to get back up

I brought it on myself

Can't blame nobody else

Then I fell on my face

And told God I needed help

Its been a long time coming

I got tired of running

He said that I could rest in His place,

But not to play in His face

So here I am

Weak in the knees, I stand

Then I drop down on 'em

To give Him all the praise that I can

"I AM that I AM", He said

"Turn from your ways & seek my refuge instead

I will increase your peace

And decrease your anguish

I will teach you new my agape love language"

With a renewed heart

And a sound mind,

I'll declare a fresh start

Along with everything that's mine

By Divine Design !

Legal Testimony

I might not be innocent
But that don't mean I can't still fight the power
I can't claim false imprisonment
But that don't mean it ain't still past the hour –
For you, for me, for us to be free
The system will drag our shit out like a tragic ass love scene
Ain't no way out of the jail unless you can afford to pay bond
Even if you really ain't do nothing – still gotta wait to be called
Other than the former, you need strings attached;
Not only that – gotta get pulled from the cardiac
Muscle head ass COs try you like a child
Public defenders do what they can to wave a fair trial
Innocence until indictment is the new norm now
Or being guilty until proven innocent in the white courthouse
There's no need to deliberate – that's what the DA say
They agree to let you out on probation (at the least)
Just so they can tie you to the state
Not to mention the fines & fees you have to pay
Jail or prison, shit is all big business
Cuz both exist with the sole intent to profit the rich
Beggars can't be choosers – they get the shit end of the stick
Poor people are usually losers in this kind of predicament
Whether you did it or not, if you got the guap, then you good
The way of the world meets the system of a down ass neighborhood
All power to the people should NOT be misunderstood
Political & spiritual warfare on every front –
The revolution BEEN begun !

HOTEP

My energy is too solid to be easily influenced by someone else's

The spirits that travel only latch on to susceptible sources

The ugly ones tend to attach themselves to weaker mortals

That's why it's important for me to strengthen myself against darker forces

Protecting my vessel by keeping down my stress levels

Meditating for manifestation to be one with my higher power

It's true what they say about these satellite towers

The processed meats & high starch foods that they feed us

In order to block the 3rd eye vision so they can better deceive us

Tactics for neutralization, yet they still need us

The energy we possess that some of us don't even know we have

If the masses are test subjects, then the world is a huge science lab

The woke ones tap in to what the sleep walkers can't even grasp

I spew my knowledge with this pen over the pad

Listen: the conspiracies are real – they did clone Tyrone

The matrix is reloaded – they got 6G for our phones

To record our brain waves when we sleep

To impress the subconscious – this shit get so deep

The spiritual & unseen forces can be so discreet

I just pray that we all find our way – Hotep AKA Peace.

SUMMER

The New Beginnings Program

Welcome to New Beginnings
Dare I speak my true feelings?
I think NOT !
I'll opt to keep my thoughts concealed –
While I praise the Most High
Singing along to songs during devotion aloud
My innermost emotions never revealed
In New Beginnings –
Where the only thing better than winning
Is staying below or above the radar
Because what you say can & probably will be
Used against you in the community meetings
Of New Beginnings
Apologizing, not even being in the wrong
But I'd do well to just let bygones be bygones
Declaring that I'm "playing" when I AIN'T;
Writing me sanctions on top of sanctions
Referring me for dismissal? LOL!
Blow the MF whistle !
We call each other "sistahs"
The spirit of togetherness must've missed us
With New Beginnings
I have no favor amongst my peers
Nor do I seek it
But don't whisper praises in my ear
And then shame me in secret
Concerning my name –
Don't even speak on it
You misread me as I am easily
Misunderstood
The way I worship is not to be looked on
Or judged
My faith does not have to be worn on my sleeve
For all to see or even to realize that its within me
Forgive me though for am NOT perfect
I can take correction or criticism
If I know I deserve it
To go back & forth anyway seems to not be worth it
It's the principle for me & the underlying purpose
About New Beginnings
Steady trynna figure out
If that's Allah looking to sharpen me
Or the devil showing out
Thank God for discernment
And Him keeping me ever in His presence
There is nothing to fear

As no man can stop my blessings
Nobody could ever run me out
Of where God has rightfully placed me
Beng put on the chopping block
Cannot shake me!
Cuz I always fall back on His security & safety
For New Beginnings –
I still hold the same sentiment
In regards to all I have expressed
But nobody will ever know it.

Reckless Endangerment

Would the desire have been so strong if I never said it out my mouth?

My burning desire

I'm liable to turn a bxtch out

I don't want the drama that comes with it

Nor do I want the sexual sickness

That's why I'll be like, "let's link up when we get free"

Learn you something new while you take this dick from me

You'll be cumming so hard, it'll make you wanfi run from me

Have you second-guessing your own sexuality

Sexual preference – sexual orientation – whatever

If you feenin' for a good pounding, I'm gon' make it hurt mo' better

If you'd rather the slow stroke, I'm cool with that too

My thrust game is strong even being up underneath you

I want your best fxck face & I'ma pull it up outta you

I'ma call you my good girl & tell you I'm proud of you

In this jail, I've been having the nastiest thoughts

The lack of sex in my life right now has got me a lil distraught

I mean I could fxck, but would I?

I'm single now, so should I?

Temptation got a hold of me

I actually like it but I should be fighting it

Because the moment I let it win,

It is then considered "reckless endangerment".

D.D.L.G.

Baby I like women

And your ass is really old enough to get it

You're just inexperienced

But when you told me parts of your fantasy

I couldn't help but to give you reassurance

That I could be exactly what you need

I can teach you how to be

A good submissive for me

A real good girl for Daddy

Don't you like to hear it?

Tickling your praise kink

It keeps me in good spirits

DDLG dynamic – baby's gotta have it

You're new to this & I'm true to this

Let's find a way to make magic

An itch is made to scratch it

Like sexing to an addict

I'm the drug & you're the fiend

You're the doll; I'm the savage

I hope you inhale my lessons deeply

Allow me to punish you on your knees

Then provide aftercare ever so sweetly

Your pleasure is my reward & treasure to you

A new lifestyle is what I'm introducing you to

Or would be if you wouldn't be leaving soon

Anyway, much love & rich blessings to you.

Mi Soon Come

Do I NOT move you?

Make you wanfi cum to me

I can soothe you

My gyal haffi run to me

Hot gyal get cool down

When she hear *my* champion sound

And I will right my wrongs

As I write this poem

Ya pum-pum fi get mash up

As soon as I get outta the slammer

Mi gon' ping-ping you like a hammer

When I come home, be ready with the camera

Mi a gon' love you fa life

I want you to be my wife

I'm finna give you all the bliss

Ya dun know everyting crisp !

FALL

Jailhouse Blues

Every jail is different, but certain things remain the same
Like the CO telling you when to eat/sleep and them calling you by your last name
Ain't been locked down for more than a week
I'm just trying to keep sane
I'm 10 toes down on my feet nigga
Still playing this mental game
And its a challenge that I manage on a daily basis
Interacting with those broken soul and smiling faces
Charges ranging anywhere from petty to murder cases
Females of many races from different places
But I ain't really thinking 'bout that though
I'm thinking bout *HER*
Our possible future together and then our last words
Was it worth it to put it together, and watch it all burn?
Her loyalty to me is my only real concern
I'm a loyal MF if she stick around to learn
If my affections are strong for her *love* gotta be firm
She gotta be a down ass bxtch for me to fully lock in
Cuz Ima switch up the play & have some hoes clock in
If I'm down on my ass, then I need like… 3 mules
Collect my cash all up & down MLK avenue
Tap in with the plug – everything gon' be okay
Ima make 2 ways when it look like no way
Ima chop the beef liver and bring home the steak
Ima light the candles *AND* blow 'em out on the cake
Ima do what I got to – whether she wanna be around or not
I know I fxcked up the plans & put us in a tight spot
What I'm trying to make up for requires alot
I just wanfi know she gon' be at the goal if I take this last shot
Oh no wait, I almost forgot what she said it was a bop on the phone
So nevermind what I stated above my love – Shalom.

Never ever have I…
Thought I would get caught up
In what seems like a setup
Did I make myself a target?
They done scaped me as the goat
Like Welcome to the Party
R.I.P. to Pop Smoke
Cuz it really ain't no joke
Y'all done took my meekness for weakness
Replaced me as Jesus
If He was alive to see this
He probably wouldn't believe it
Peace be upon him
For Allah knows the reason
And He is *still* with me in this tough & trying season
I will not play victim
But I feel so conflicted
If you think I'm being wronged
Then help me in my affliction
Cuz I ain't Jesus 4real
I was just supposed to portray him
Got me feeling like some of y'all Judas
When he proceeded to betray him
Kiss me on my cheek
And tell me everything sweet
"Oh you doing better Curry"
"You ain't got no need to worry"
In so many ways that is correct
I'm well protected & God has never neglected
To show me what I desire to see
When I ask to be shown indeed
So that I can move accordingly
They try to prey on me
But I'ma wolf, not a sheep
A lone one at that cuz I don't run in a pack
I roam alone & I'm loyal
And when I return to the dust,
It'll be to some of the richest soil
I wasn't cut from the same cloth
Like alot of y'all – I ain't no snake or sloth
Like that, nah, I do not transform
The Georgia peach cannot compete with the Florida orange
A peach is tasty but an orange packed with vitamins & nutrients
I'ma bring life – WTF is y'all doing?

Steady plotting, waiting on another woman's ruin?
Voo-dooing – but <u>not</u> in a good way
Whether they hate it or love it for me
(Mentally, emotionally, physically, spiritually)
I am in a good space.

The Dismissal (The Disrespect)

Tired of all this hoe shit
Dry-snitching & some mo' shit
Y'all be doing the most shit!
But I be acting like I don't know shit
Bxtches in here be having me flabbergasted
Ya'lld be mad if I slap fye off y'all asses
Stop with the cop city shit!
Policing ass hoes –
I be done snatched off yo titty bih !
Be done wrote me sanctions for saying
"Nigga this" & "nigga that"
I say "nigga" 46 times a day
Nigga, how 'bout that?
I'm solid asF – no cap
And because I'm not a rat
Spilling tea, gossip, and slander
I guess I don't meet y'all standards
Of the new beginnings propaganda.

Introspection

When I'm quiet, I'm writing
Even if it's in my head
My poetry inciting
Resurrection from the dead
With God's grace,
I command my space
Hateful words better left unsaid
I must stop & think
Before I speak
As I'd rather not cause dread
Also being mindful of the company I keep
I shall protect my crown & wash my feet
The snakes at the gates will all be chopped
My walking in authority cannot be stopped
I may wobble & stumble here and there,
Though it is NOT to my despair
I find confidence in the strength
That God inherently blesses me with
And so it is written
Already for my descendants
To manifest the best
With the anointing that has been given
And nothing less.